How to Stop Lying

The Ultimate Cure Guide for Pathological Liars and Compulsive Liars

Table of Contents

Introduction

The pages in this short book were developed through years of experiences that I have had, as well as what has been proven to work for others that I have talked to and researched. I also want to congratulate you for taking the time to understand pathological/compulsive lying, whether it is for yourself or to help out somebody that you know who may be dealing with this.

This short, detailed book is aimed to help people who want to better understand how a compulsive liar thinks, signs of a compulsive liar, how compulsive liars become that way in the first place, as well as strategies to overcome compulsive lying.

People who suffer from compulsive lying have a tendency to hide their problems from friends, family, and even their doctors. As a result, there is not much information to work with regarding ways to treat it directly. But the available treatments so far target the need to change habits and manage emotions in order to stop the compulsion. That is what you will find in this book.

I can guarantee that you will find this book useful if you make sure to implement what you learn in the following pages. The important thing is that you IMPLEMENT what you learn. Compulsive lying is not conquered overnight, but the important thing to remember is that it is definitely possible for you to overcome it. What I am giving you is the information so that you can understand your own mind and thinking, as well as the steps you will need to make that journey.

As you go through these pages, you'll get a better understanding of what compulsive lying really is, where it stems from, and you will learn several ways that you can begin to overcome it. We will dive into what is going on in your brain, how your mind reacts to your triggers, how your early childhood can influence the rest of your life, as well as what work is required of you to get past the roadblocks that are in your way.

I recommend that you take notes while you read this book to ensure that you get the most out of the information in here. I want you to look over the notes of this book even after you've finished reading it. The notes will help you to pinpoint exactly what you need to implement, and by writing things down, you will be able to recall specifics and how to handle certain situations when they arise.

Lastly, remember that everything in this book has been compiled through research, my own experiences, as well as the experiences of others, so feel free to question what you have read in this book. I encourage you to do your own research on the things that you want to look deeper into.

The more you understand about your own mind and body, the better off you'll be. To overcome compulsive lying, it will take some work on your part but you can do it! So remember to read with confidence   and   an   open   mind!

Chapter 1:

What Are Pathological/Compulsive Liars?

Compulsive liars and *pathological liars* are terms that are often used interchangeably to refer to someone who lies out of habit. Telling a lie for the average person is usually accompanied with a sense of guilt.

Because of this, lying can be difficult for most people. However, there are some people who have more trouble telling the truth than telling a lie.

Difference Between Compulsive and Pathological Lying

Depending on how long the person has been a compulsive liar, he/she may not even be conscious that they are continuing to lie for pointless reasons. They have become so used to lying that it becomes second nature to them.

Compulsive lying usually comes from experiences where one feels that lying is a necessity, such as defending themselves from a bully, or hiding the truth to protect someone else.

Because of experiences that make compulsive liars feel that hiding the truth will make them feel better, they feel that telling the truth is very unsatisfactory. As a result, they opt to lie about anything at all, until it becomes an automatic response. However, this does not necessarily mean that the liar has any conscious intention of manipulating or taking advantage of other people.

Pathological liars, on the other hand, have an entirely different motivation when it comes to lying. These liars feel that their ability to bend the truth is a skill that they can use for their personal benefit. Their lying does not come from an experience or a positive intention, and these people are capable of lying without any feeling of remorse or guilt.

If they think that they have gotten away with a lie, they will experience satisfaction from the idea that they were able to fool someone. Many pathological liars even experience a thrill from being able to fool others. Pathological liars will usually never admit to their lies and will be ready to defend themselves to anyone who questions what comes out of their mouth.

Although pathological lying is not yet recognized as a mental disorder, many psychologists agree that habitual lying can be a sign of deeper psychological problems. Pathological liars develop the habit of lying at some point in their life, usually in their early childhood years when their brain is very susceptible to picking up new habits, whether they are beneficial or not.

If a child realizes he/she is able to get away with lying at a very young age and finds it beneficial to survival, he/she usually will not stop without intervention. Because these habits get reinforced as the child grows, confronting a young child about a lie can be very beneficial to the developing mind, while trying to confront a grown adult about their habitual lying can be very painful, because of factors such as pride and low self-esteem.

Liars Start Out Young

When you attempt to look deeper into the act of lying, it is also important to see what people really get out of telling something that is far from the truth. At this point, you may even see that the core reason is simple: lying has always allowed people to prevent themselves from getting into conflicts that they are not prepared to face. These conflicts, of course, become increasingly complex as a person matures into adulthood.

A child, for example, would want to escape the conflict that he/she may have with parents if they find out that he/she was not able to meet their expectations. Of course, that child would also want to avoid the loss of some privileges that he/she enjoys if only they were able to do what these authority figures expected from them. If not fixing his/her bed means not being allowed to use the gaming console for the entire weekend, then that child begins to formulate in his/her mind that it just might be alright to lie for such an obvious gain.

What happens when a person learns how to lie and get away with it? That person begins to feel that there are no moral clauses attached to the very act of lying. Because people often tolerate children telling tall stories or stealing cookies, young people often form a logical conclusion that it is alright to lie. People may call them out for telling lies, but if they can deny that accusation, they realize that they will not be severely punished anyway.

By lying as a defense mechanism and realizing that one can get away with it, a person may begin to lose the remorse that another person who would otherwise feel guilty when lying, would have. This lack of guilt can develop over a long period of time, where a person progressively feels less and less guilt while lying, because their mind is observing that the person can get away with this behavior without any real consequences.

If you know someone who is a compulsive liar, it is important to understand this slow erosion of guilt so that you can better sympathize with them. If you are a person that has a young child, it's important to teach them why the behavior of lying can be detrimental in life, so that they associate the act of lying with feelings that are unpleasant.

Our formative years as infants, toddlers, and young children will always be very difficult for us to see objectively in hindsight - even with all the details. Fortunately or unfortunately, this is also a time where we develop character habits and quirky behaviors that become "ingrained" in our personality. As we age, especially during late teenage years and early adulthood, we slowly but surely learn to see the occurrences in our lives through a more objective lens.

To make matters worse, children may also see adult/authority figures telling lies and getting away with them. As a person grows into an adult, he/she may also see that the world that they are living in has actually tolerated lying in one way or another, and that the only way for a person to avoid being punished for lying is to deny it or avoid getting caught.

While we'll always have our own personal biases in the way we perceive the triggers for our behaviors and the way they affect others, we also learn more about subjects like psychology, sociology, social norms, and how we are perceived by others. This is also why children can get away with lying relatively easily compared to when they are older teenagers and adults.

Oftentimes, teenage or adult peers will "call out" the behavior, and the compulsive liar starts to see how this behavior is being perceived by others. By combining the way we "feel" intuitively with our life experiences, our knowledge of human behavior, and our own personal tendencies, we can begin to see the things that happen to us in a clearer, less obstructed view.

Oftentimes, if a person continues to lie about many things in their life for a span of years, they are not able to develop true self-esteem regarding the issues they lied about. This can handicap them later in life because if they decide to try and overcome their compulsive lying, they find it even more difficult because they don't know who they are without the imaginary character of themselves that they have built up in their head. At this point, many people find it easier to just stick with their old habit of lying instead of facing the dark reality of dealing with a low perceived self-worth.

Furthermore, many psychologists believe that compulsive liars are trying to deceive themselves as much as they are trying to fool others. They want to believe their lies and are often convinced of them. Some experts speculate that lying is one of the techniques people use to disguise their insecurities and low self-esteem. Compulsive liars, on the other hand, may even desire to push deception to another level by practicing to make their body language disguise the lies that they tell others.

For this reason, those who will do whatever it takes to lie will be able to fool polygraph tests and their psychiatrists as well. In the end, if a pathological liar does not voluntarily go through evaluation and become committed to changing his/her life, then that person usually will not receive the treatment they truly need.

In conclusion, pathological lying is one of the first symptoms exhibited by people with diagnosed mental illnesses. It is also often correlated to personality disorder and narcissistic disorder, though further research is still being conducted on this subject in order to better   classify.

Chapter 2:

Why Do We Lie?

Whether you are a pathological liar or someone you know is, it is extremely important that you understand that all humans lie. Yes, all humans lie. Each and every one of us lies for what WE THINK are the best of reasons.

The truth is, 90% of children understand the concept of lying by the age of four, when they immediately feel that truth omission can actually bring benefits. At an early age, children know that they may get toys, snacks and many other things that they like if they start saying things that make adults feel compelled to give out rewards to them.

As people get older, their needs become increasingly more complex, which prompts them to lie even more. In a 2002 study done by the University of Massachusetts, lying by adults is as severe as having 60% of them unable to go through a 10 minute conversation without sprinkling in at least one lie or extreme exaggeration.

Who Do We Lie To?

According to studies, most people do not generally lie about big things. Often, people are inclined to lie about things that do not matter that much and would be compelled to lie to look better in front of others. People are also more prone to lying to those who are constantly around them.

In a survey conducted by a British company, 30% of those who responded to their study lied about seeing the movie Godfather. Why do people lie about such a small thing? Because telling people that you have watched a classic film is very likely to make you a more like-able person.

The Day America Told the Truth has a rundown of statistics on who gets the bulk of people's lies in this country. In this study, they found out that

89% of the population is likely to lie to their parents. 75% of people lie to their friends. About 69% of spouses also lie to their partners. If you are looking for love on an online dating app, then you are likely to read a lie in a profile approximately 90% of the time.

Types of Lies People Often Commit

1) White Lies

White lies are often seen as the most innocent of lies since the underlying motivation for telling them springs out of courtesy or politeness. For example, if you tell someone that you appreciate the gift that he/she brought you during your party, even if you don't, you think that you made your guest feel comfortable by denying them the truth.

However, this does not mean that white lies can never bring about conflict. Over time, it can drive people away because they may soon realize that you are insincere with the good gestures that you are showing to them.

For this reason, there is a great tendency that you will lose your credibility once people discover your lies. At the same time, telling white lies may also create a major roadblock when it comes having deeper and trusting relationship with another person.

2) Broken Promises

A broken promise means failure to keep one's commitment to another person. It is often delivered to avoid conflict or to gain personal advantage. Since promises often sound like a good deal to a person that has been promised to, most people enter these compromises to get something that they want or need, even if they are not sure that they will be able to keep their word.

You can think of these as verbal collateral to a loan that you do not intend to pay, while making sure that the other party provides the full investment that you expect.

Broken promises are very damaging, not only to the person who gives them, but especially to the person who has devoted his/her time to believing that the other party will fulfill their end of the bargain. If a broken promise requires a bigger investment from a person, then it may even lead to disrupting one's daily life.

3) Outright Lies

You can think of an outright lie as a bold-faced lie that you tell other people, even though everyone knows that you are not telling the truth.

When a child tells you that he did not eat chocolate even though you see that his entire mouth is smeared by the food that he denies he ate, then you are being told an outright lie.

As people grow older, they become increasingly more clever when it comes to giving out these lies. However, some people eventually get caught and even though there is clear evidence that implicates them, they still insist that they are telling the truth.

This makes other people feel that they are wasting their time and energy in confronting a liar. In addition, they might feel that an outright liar is belittling their intelligence.

4) Exaggerations

Exaggerations happen when you tell something that is true, but do not stick to the way events really happened – instead, you blow details out of proportion. For example, if you tell someone that your friend is extremely mad at them, instead of sticking to the truth that your friend is just a little frustrated at the person you are talking to, then this is considered a lie in the form of exaggeration.

Exaggeration is a mix of truth and lie, and for those people who love committing them, these weavings of fact and fiction make them look a lot more impressive to others. It is also likely that exaggerators may end up believing the fibs that they have made up since they are still connected to the truth.

5) Fabrications

Fabrications work similarly to gossip. They are created to appear as facts about another person or situation, without verification if they are true or not.

Oftentimes, fabrications work against their subjects, and are often delivered with the intention of maligning them.

6) Deceptive Lies

These lies are often committed by those who have the intention of making people think that they are someone who they are really not. For example, if you are telling people that you are an astronaut when you are not, then you are deceiving people into thinking that you are someone with a particular skill set or background.

Deception always comes with a motive – you would want to make people believe that you are more important than what they think, which ultimately lures them into believing that they can trust you with certain tasks, or make them want to give you better opportunities that you would never otherwise get if they knew who you really were.

However, deceivers are easily caught, especially if they cannot exhibit qualities or knowledge of the person that they are pretending to be.

7) Lies of Omission

Some people believe that these lies do not count, since they told something true anyway. However, omitting a part of the truth considered a lie since it means leaving out substantial portions of the story that will give results that are opposite to what one expects.

8) Plagiarism

This is not only an act of lying, but also an act of stealing. Plagiarism entails claiming another work as one's own. Without crediting the rightful owner of a piece of work, one can get the benefit of getting another person's profit or credit.

9) Lies of Personification

These lies work like lies of omission in such a way that the person who commits them only tells a portion of the truth by making a claim to who he/she is as a person. However, this does not necessarily make it true that he/she did not do something or became someone that they are trying to deny.

For example, if someone asks you "Do you eat the fat off the barbecue?" and you respond with "I am a bikini model!", it does not necessarily mean that you don't eat fatty meat at all times.

Reasons Why People Lie

All adults and kids omit or distort the truth for five main situations that we find ourselves in. All lies fall somewhere into these five categories.

These are to: avoid hurting someone; avoid feeling guilt or shame; avoid conflict and stress (minor to major); gain a social advantage; and avoid a significant loss.

Avoid Hurting Someone

To many people, this is considered a nobler reason to lie compared to the others. This is, perhaps, the type of lying that people would be most lenient about if they were to find out that a person committed this type of lie to them.

An example of lying to avoid hurting someone would be if your spouse asked you if you thought that he/she was overweight and you lied to protect his/her feelings by telling them what would make them feel better, rather than giving your honest opinion.

Another more extreme example would be if you were to find someone bullying another person and made up a lie in order to spare the person who was getting bullied. In both cases, the liar would be committing a lie because they thought, at the time, that it would be best to lie in order to avoid hurting someone involved in the situation.

Some people think that removing portions of the truth, or deceiving another person to prevent him/her from getting hurt is acceptable because the other party will never be able to accept the truth.

However, this often prevents the other person from forming well-informed opinions about the situation they really are in. At the same time, it can cause the other party to experience more hurt, especially when he/she finds out that they have been acting and reacting based on wrong information.

Avoid Feeling Guilt or Shame

Lying to avoid feeling guilt or shame is especially common in the family dynamic of a child-parent relationship. An example would be if a parent told their child, every day, that it is unacceptable to receive any grade lower than a "B" in their classes at school.

If the child came home with a "C" grade in a class, that child may begin to feel shame or guilt about what had happened. This might encourage the child to think of lying in order to avoid the pain associated with the parent possibly yelling at them, grounding them, or punishing them in some other form.

To the child, it could be a better option just to lie, based on how they perceive the situation to be. This pattern can form from a young age and can definitely develop as the child grows older. If this continues for many years, it can result in the child lying to the parent several times a day, even if there is no perceived benefit to some of the lies being told.

Again, the reason an older child could potentially continue lying to their parent, even if there is no perceived benefit, is because the habit of lying in the relationship has already been established as acceptable - even if it is subconscious.

In the end, a person who lies because of guilt or shame makes it a point to create a more satisfying environment, instead of exploring other options that will actually be healthier for him/her. Avoiding exposure to guilt or shame prevents a person from acknowledging their mistakes and developing the understanding that they have the right to be accepted for who they really   are.

Avoid Conflict and Stress

The previous example could fall under this category as well. Lying to avoid conflict and stress is oftentimes used in a situation where family members or close friends are involved. A person might want to keep a relationship intact and feels that the best way to preserve that relationship, without conflict, is to tell a lie in order to keep all parties happy.

In many situations, a person would rather not risk losing the relationship by saying what is really on their mind. The problem that can come up with this line of reasoning, however, is that it becomes very difficult later on to develop a deep, authentic relationship because the foundation that the relationship was built on was not transparent to begin with.

Gain A Social Advantage

The fourth situation people tend to lie in would be for gaining a social advantage. This type of lying is becoming more and more common in today's world because we are becoming a society that is becoming dependent on reputation. Lying to gain a social advantage can really benefit a person to get more out of the world then they would otherwise be able to get, if they were in a different social class or lower in the professional ranks, with less opportunities.

An example of this can be seen in the dating world. A man or woman who is looking to date someone who he/she may see as a little beyond his/her socioeconomic class, might try to impress by lying about social status. This could include their profession, how much money they earn, and/or some of their hobbies.

A person in this situation may think that these actions could possibly help them out in the long run. Again, like the last example, if this becomes a habit, the person lying could run the risk of never developing a strong romantic relationship with another person because they aren't laying the foundation correctly for a transparent relationship.

Gaining social advantage is also usually the goal of compulsive liars since it allows them to expand their circle and deceive other people for personal gain.

Avoid Significant Losses

The last of the five reasons is lying to avoid significant losses. A practical example of this would be if someone were to lie on their taxes about how much income they received in order to keep more money and to avoid "losing money" to the government.

Somebody lying in this situation might have many reasons to do so, such as feeling like the government is asking for too much, or maybe they feel like they need the money to survive.

Either way, the person feels that their lie is the right thing to do at the time because of their current situation. They might feel like it will only be a one-time occurrence or that it will be harmless, but just like all small lies, it can become repetitive and the consequences can steepen as time passes.

Lying to prevent a loss, however, prevents a person from truly facing the consequences in the situation that they are currently in. When a person turns to lying to escape his/her situation, the person becomes trapped in a cycle of denying the situation without developing any means to truly solve his/her problems.

Ultimately, when people lie and get caught, they often reason that everybody is doing it anyway. Take any study about lying and you will see that most people see this act as natural. Since people think that everybody lies anyway, they think that others should be lenient to them in any event that they were to get caught.

Compulsive liars usually do not see that lying can go a long way when it comes to damaging themselves and other people. Because they view lying as a means to an end, they provide all the justifications that they need to get off the hook.

However, the first thing that these liars need to do is to realize that their actions carry a huge weight on their future and that people around them can only tolerate their actions up to a certain point.

This means that they should learn that lying is not really a dilemma that they should forget about when they manage to pull off their lies, but an action that will bring them the losses that they were trying to avoid in the first place.

Chapter 3:

Signs and Symptoms

If you are unsure whether you have the tendencies of a pathological liar, here are the common traits of pathological/compulsive liars that researchers have come to conclusions on. Since pathological lying is not technically considered a disorder, it does not have a list of symptoms.

However, pathological liars do exhibit common traits. Understanding the signs of a pathological liar will help people identify if they, or someone they know, is already suffering from habitual lying.

Constant Attention-Seeking in Interactions

One of the main reasons why pathological liars try to deceive people is so they can be the center of attention. By being able to twist the events of a story, or by building up a larger than life persona, a pathological liar is able to get attention from others that they may not otherwise receive.

These people usually crave the attention that others give them, which pushes them to lie even more in the future. It becomes a cycle, where the liar becomes addicted to the rush from the reactions of the people they communicate with.

Some people also tend to tell lies whenever they realize that someone is getting the spotlight that is supposed to be for them, causing them to feel that they need to compete with those who are stealing the show from them. You may spot this narcissistic behavior from people who are butting in on conversations, telling everyone that they have the same story as the other person - but they have a better version. You may also notice these people cutting others out mid-sentence to tell their "amazing" story.

Telling Impossible Stories

A great way to spot a pathological liar is to pay attention to the types of stories they tell about themselves when you aren't there to witness the events. Pathological liars will oftentimes tell unbelievable stories that can even seem pointless.

While all people can exaggerate their stories from time to time, pathological liars do it out of habit rather than really thinking about what they will benefit from by making such an outlandish story. They may do it to make themselves look more adventurous, or to make themselves look more skillful than they really are. Sometimes, they even make it a point to "adopt" the skills of other people in their stories to make theirs' more compelling.

If you begin to notice that the way someone acts in the stories is much different than the way you see them act when you are spending time with them, it is a sign that he/she may be a pathological liar.

If you find that a person is telling a story that is too good to be true, or you find that your jaw is dropping every time that person tells a story, then you have a reason to think that he/she may be lying, at least at a certain degree. Pathological liars are known to be incapable of resisting the urge to twist every actual story into a better, fictional one.

Making Every Situation Seem Easy

Some compulsive liars will never admit that they are having difficulty handling the circumstances in their life. Instead, they may only discus happy incidents or make up stories to cover unfortunate events. This form of lying is common for habitual liars.

We all go through difficult, trying times throughout our lives and, although it is beneficial to be optimistic most of the time, many compulsive liars will resist admitting that they are having trouble handling a tough situation, even with a close friend or family member, because they don't want to be seen as being vulnerable to others.

They may want to avoid the feeling of embarrassment, or being caught in a lie that they may have previously told their friends about how well they are living their lives. They may feel that admitting that they are going through tough times will cause other people to think of them as weak or incapable.

Portraying Themselves as Victims

On the other hand, some pathological liars may portray themselves as victims in order to garner attention from others. People who are always sick or portraying themselves constantly as the victim may either be very unlucky or a pathological liar. If a person continues to make up horrible stories all the time, it is a sign that he/she is a pathological liar.

You may be thinking, how would I know if the person is unlucky or really a liar? The key is to pay attention to how their stories are phrased. If a person is always making his/herself out to seem like the victim of their story rather than just talking about an unfortunate situation from an objective viewpoint, you might have your answer. We all go through rough patches, but trying to avoid all blame is a tell-tale sign.

Some people, on the other hand, take their need to get attention to the next level. Doctors, for example, face patients who have developed Munchausen Syndrome, or the disorder that creates a strong desire to have a physical or mental disability to make people think that they are difficult to understand.

Some people come to clinics and deliberately produce HIV results in blood tests, or even attempt to mix blood with their urine samples. Because they seek to be cared for, they go to all these lengths to portray themselves as victims.

Having Poor Self-Esteem

Pathological liars will lie in order to feel better about themselves, whether it is about their looks, their accomplishments, or their family life. If someone has become a pathological liar, it usually means that they felt insecure about a specific area of their life at some point, and over time, they developed the habit of lying about it to avoid facing the insecurity head-on.

Pathological liars tend to deny the world that they live in; instead of accepting who they really are, they want to live in a fantasy world where people are compelled to be attracted to them or respect them. Since they feel that it does not happen in real life, they find that twisting the truth is their recourse to get what they want. However, it is also important for people to recognize that pathological lying may be a cry for help, for people to accept the person for who they really are.

Chapter 4:

How to Finally Stop Lying

If you have come to the conclusion that you have tendencies of a pathological liar and are sure that you want to overcome these tendencies, it is important to understand a very key piece of information: To stop compulsive lying, you will need to put in a lot of time and effort.

Breaking the Habit

If you are aware that you are lying out of habit, then the first thing that you need to do is to figure out how to break this behavior. To prevent yourself from lying, you need to be sure whether you are lying or not.

Remember that you need to be fully committed to stop this habit or change your life, or else you will simply win against any polygraph test even when you know that you are undergoing one to help yourself. Without willingly going through treatment or therapy with the full admission that you do have a problem, you will easily lie to any physician or psychiatrist who is willing to handle your case.

You will essentially need to rewire your behavior. Over time, your brain develops patterns and links experiences together, in order to help you navigate through the world in the most efficient way possible. If you began compulsive lying at a young age, think about how many years your brain has been complying with that pattern of thinking.

An unfortunate fact about why most pathological liars have been lying for so long is that they may have never had a person really sit down with them and call them out on their behavior. If a person has gotten away with lying for years, then their brain begins to accept the action as perfectly acceptable because it is helping the person go through life without conflict.

So the key here is to remember that it took many years to get to this point and it will take time to rewire your brain to recognize the patterns that you want it to. The amount of time it takes to change your habit is based a great deal on how much you want to immerse yourself in the process of overcoming it and how important it is to you. At the end of the day, you must decide what you value more in the long run - the truth or pleasing others.

Your habitual lying provides you with dopamine bursts that you've become addicted to. In essence, the false self-image that you've created with your lies, is rewarded each time you bring it up. If your constructed false self-image is complimented, you will begin to find yourself more attached to it, making it more difficult to eventually overcome it. The more you lie about a specific area of your life, the stronger your will-power will need to be to eventually override the false beliefs/persona.

Telling the truth habitually will create new neural pathways, making you more likely to default to a truthful response in the future. As you progressively re-wire your behavior to be truthful as the default, you should create positive, empowering beliefs and constructive, compounding habits to replace the previous ones.

The ego and false self-image works in the short-term, but humility allows for long-term growth and acceptance. Oftentimes, we give "alternate truths" because we want to appear "interesting", "successful", or "having everything under control" because we haven't embraced being vulnerable and trusting of others. In essence, you have probably built shields around yourself in order to avoid criticism and pain from others' reactions to you.

Nevertheless, once a person admits that he/she is a pathological liar, the next problem that they will inevitably encounter is how to ask for help. It is hard enough for pathological liars to admit to themselves that they are compulsively lying, so talking to someone else about it will be even more of a challenge.

All treatments for pathological lying must be done voluntarily. In the following pages, I am going to give you many ways to overcome your compulsive lying. Some of these are exercises you can do through therapy; others you will be able to do with a close friend, family member, or even by yourself. I am going to describe them as done with a therapist so that if you want to do them by yourself or with a close friend, you can substitute the therapist with the person you have in mind.

As mentioned before, the best way to overcome your compulsive lying is to commit as much of yourself as you can and to use as many of the techniques as possible, at the same time, in order to get optimal results.

Even if a person goes through counseling and therapy, if they do not believe that they have a problem, treatment will be ineffective. Pathological liars who are unable to realize their problems will usually end their therapy or lie about feeling better just to end the treatment.

Therapy is a common treatment for pathological liars; it is accompanied by a professional diagnosis to determine if a person has a deeper mental illness. The duration of the treatment depends on each case. There are many underlying issues that a pathological liar has to address in order to get better, and psychologists can help patients get through the process quicker than if done independently.

Psychotherapy is a therapy that involves an interaction between the patient and the therapist that relies on psychological principles to help pathological liars change their behaviors. During psychotherapy, you are able to express your deep-seated thoughts without having to worry about being judged or ridiculed.

Skillful therapists are good listeners; although pathological liars might try to lie their way through the therapy, a good psychologist will be able to identify these deceptions. Be open to the conversation that the therapist is initiating. Remember that they are only trying to help you uncover the reasons for your compulsive lying and have no reason to judge you.

An ethical therapist will not promise any overnight results to cure pathological lying but they do instill hope that, with combined effort from you and your support system, you can overcome pathological lying for good.

Psychologists use different approaches to provide encouragement and hope for their clients. The display of empathy and attentiveness may already be a good form of therapy.

If you are looking to get help through therapy, the following information provides helpful advice to make sure that you receive the appropriate care that you need:

1) Seek recommendations from respected sources, such as physicians, family members, or others who have overcome issues with lying. You can also ask for referrals from medical centers since they know who the licensed therapists are.

2) Ask inquiries about the services that the therapists offer. Be careful with professionals who advertise too much and claim that they can cure all problems without any work on your part. Also, make sure that the therapist is a licensed medical professional. Be sure to inquire about the success rates of individuals who have undergone the same treatments.

3) Once a formal evaluation has been completed, discuss the treatment plan before making a commitment to it. If you have doubts about the treatment plan, do not be afraid to state your concerns. An ethical professional will be willing to address any issues their clients have.

4) Be sure to request a second opinion if you are still unsure about the first therapist.

Psychodynamic Therapy

Sigmund Freud pioneered a model of psychotherapy called the psychoanalysis. This treatment aims to help people who are suffering from psychological disorders by gaining insight into the internal conflicts that lie at the root cause of pathological lying. Psychodynamic therapists believe that by working through a person's conflicts, they will be able to free themselves from their unconscious need to protect themselves through lies.

According to the principles of psychodynamic therapy, pathological lying is just a way for people to shield themselves from their inner turmoil. In essence, it promotes the idea that by solving the root cause of the behavior, people will no longer feel the desire to lie.

Psychodynamic therapy can help you to become more aware of the deep causes of your pathological lying and you might even change your outlook on life after undergoing it. There are three major methods within psychodynamic therapy. These include: free association, dream analysis, and transference.

Free Association

Free association is when a person utters thoughts as they come to mind. You will be encouraged to say what is on your mind whether it would be considered "appropriate" or not.

Being able to express yourself uncensored will gradually break down your defenses. Initially, most liars will show resistance and will only discuss matters they want to talk about.

Although most free association therapies begin with small talk, the compulsion to utter can convince pathological liars to disclose more meaningful information as time goes on.

Dream Analysis

Sigmund Freud believed that people lower their defenses while dreaming, but because defenses may not be totally eliminated, impulses may take a symbolized form. Psychoanalysts believe that dreams have two levels of content: manifest and latent content.

The manifest content is the actual dream that a person experiences. The latent content is the unconscious manifestation or the symbolism of the dream. The interpretation of the dream may vary from person to person, so the therapist may ask to free associate with the patient in order to understand the latent content.

Transference

Clients may respond to their therapist, not only as a medical professional, but also as an important figure in their lives. A client may see their therapist as a motherly figure or as a close friend. The process of analyzing transference relationships is an important part of psychoanalysis.

Pathological liars may be unconsciously channeling their real emotions towards their therapist, and this can help them resolve their issues. Transference therapy generally takes a long time, sometimes even lasting for years. However, it can be one of, if not the most, fulfilling relationship for a person who is dealing with compulsive lying.

Behavioral Therapy

Behavioral therapy is a systematic approach, where the focus is to change the behavior of the patient and not to change their personality or to uncover their past. Behavioral therapy can last for only a few weeks to a few months.

Therapists believe that the efficiency of behavioral therapy is derived from learned techniques rather than from the establishment of therapeutic relationships.

Behavioral therapy was first used to treat phobias and other behaviors that have been resistant to other forms of traditional therapy. Pathological liars can undergo behavioral therapy only if they are prepared to face their fears. Behavioral therapy includes methods like systematic desensitization, gradual exposure, and modeling.

Systematic Desensitization

This is a therapeutic program that involves being constantly exposed to a fearful stimulus. First, the patient is asked to undergo a relaxation technique, then they are instructed to imagine scenes that they might be uncomfortable being involved in. In the case of pathological liars, this may be a scene where they have no option but to tell the truth.

The patient will be asked to focus on restoring their relaxation whenever fear is evoked. This procedure is undergone until the patient is able to imagine previously frightful scenes without panicking.

Gradual Exposure

Gradual exposure involves a compulsive liar actually being exposed to his/her fears. This may involve speaking the truth in front of other people or admitting that the person has been lying to their friends.

The therapy progresses at the pace of the patient, and it can also be combined with cognitive techniques to replace anxious thoughts with calm thoughts.

Modeling

Modeling is a therapy where a patient tries to emulate certain desired behaviors. A pathological liar may be asked to imitate other cured pathological liars. After observing the model, they will be assisted in performing the behavior.

It is important to visualize the type of person you will be when you stop lying - from the interactions you have to the thoughts that run through your head.

Imagine yourself saying the true things that you would say in certain situations with your friends and other people you come into contact with. This goes back to the rewiring of the brain and has been shown to be effective.

Chapter 5:

Humanistic Therapy and Group Therapy

While most psychodynamic therapists focus on the unconscious processes of the brain, humanistic therapists focus on their patients' conscious experiences.

There are also similarities between psychotherapy and humanistic therapy. Both treatments assume that a person's past has something to do with their present behavior.

Person-Centered Therapy

Person-centered therapy was first developed by Carl Rogers. Rogers believed that disorders like pathological lying were caused by roadblocks that people experienced in their path towards self-actualization.

According to Rogers, pathological liars may have started to lie because they sought out approval from their peers, and so they wore a mask and lied about who they were and what they experienced.

Eventually, pathological liars would become unaware of their own inner voices and develop a distorted self-concept. As a result, these individuals believed their own lies and experienced difficulty in trying to own up to the truth.

Person-centered therapy creates an environment where pathological liars are able to accept their true selves. The therapy is non-directive, which means that the patient, rather than the therapist, will be the one who leads the progress of the treatment.

In this model, the therapist will rephrase whatever the patient expresses without passing any judgment. This will allow a pathological liar to explore the feelings that have been buried under their lies.

Cognitive Therapy

Cognitive therapists may help pathological liars identify and correct their faulty thinking and attitude that results in their compulsive need to lie. Let's explore these options:

Rational Emotive Behavioral Therapy

Some therapists believe that the lies made up by pathological liars are brought about by their irrational belief that they must have the approval of most of the people around them.

Although it is understandable to want other people's admiration, it is considered irrational if a person thinks he/she cannot live without it.

In rational emotive behavioral therapy, therapists dispute the irrational beliefs of their patients and help them to develop an alternative belief. The therapists will help pathological liars find a more desirable outlet rather than lying.

Beck's Cognitive Therapy

Through this treatment, pathological liars will be asked to recognize and change the errors in their thinking. They will be asked to record instances in which they feel the urge to lie. The therapist then disputes distorted thoughts and replaces them with rational alternatives.

Another type of cognitive therapy is creating a reality in which a patient can test out their negative beliefs in real-life situations. For example, if a pathological liar believes that no one will like him/her if he/she does not invent incredible stories, that person can test out that theory and call his/her friends and tell them a story that really happened. In many cases, the person might be surprised to learn that the people in his/her life appreciate real stories better than lies.

Cognitive Behavioral Treatment

Cognitive behavioral treatment uses therapeutic techniques to change the patient's thoughts and behaviors. Cognitive behavioral treatment assumes that the change in a person's thinking patterns and beliefs will produce desirable changes in their behavior.

Therapists use different behavioral techniques to correct automatic thought patterns that may trigger pathological lying. Cognitive behavioral treatments have an impressive record of treating pathological lying and other emotional disorders, such as stress disorders, socio-phobia, and even personality disorders.

Eclectic Therapy

Eclectic therapy uses multiple approaches to achieve therapeutic benefits. For example, they can use behavioral therapy to entice change in a pathological liar's behavior and incorporate psychodynamic therapy in order to gain insight into the patient's past and the cause of the lying.

According to some sources, an increasing number of patients react better to eclectic therapy than other treatments. Eclectic therapists tend to be older and more experienced than most therapists and have learned, through experience, how to incorporate different methods to cure pathological lying.

Group Therapy

Group therapy has many advantages, one being less individual costs because several people are being treated at the same time. Some experts also believe that it is easier to treat a group of patients who have the same problem because of the community feel.

Some people may opt for a treatment that involves groups of people, families, and even couples. This can work well if the person feels comfortable enough to be open about their issues with lying and is looking for accountability and connection.

This enables pathological liars to learn how other people with the same problems cope with their behavioral issues. It can also strengthen the support system for the individual patients. The group may also practice situational events in which pathological liars are encouraged to change their ways.

Family Therapy

Unfortunately, pathological lying can cause emotional distress for a liar's family. Family therapy aims to help the members of the family resolve their conflicts. This can help them communicate with each other without the need for lies.

Oftentimes, it is unavoidable for families to blame the pathological liar for their family's problems. These families sometimes seem to believe that by changing the behavior of the pathological liar, their family will be able to function properly again.

However, family therapists encourage all members of the family to work together to resolve conflicts and to not make the pathological liar feel too guilty, as long as he/she is making progress.

Couple Therapy

This therapy is best used for couples who are dealing with at least one member who is a pathological liar. Couple therapy focuses on improving truthful communication between each partner.

It is especially helpful if one or both of the partners are realizing that the pathological lying is beginning to take a toll on the relationship, but still believe that the relationship can still be saved.

Chapter 6:

More Techniques and Tips

After a person commits to ending their habit, they can gradually free themselves from the lies that held them down for so long. However, just like any treatment, therapy for pathological liars takes time and dedication to ensure that the person does not relapse into their old ways.

Here are a few more techniques and tips that have worked for me and that professionals in the field recommend:

Subliminal Messages to Honesty

Listening and watching subliminal messages specifically created for pathological liars will be helpful. By subjecting yourself to repeated messages, you won't even be aware of the changes that happen deep within your subconscious mind.

This is great for the rewiring of your brain that we were covering earlier. A great way to do this is to set an alarm for every hour or every few hours and right when the alarm goes off, read a message out loud to yourself.

Your brain will begin to see this pattern and it will help you to speed up the process. A great message you can read to yourself would be something like, "Whatever I say has value simply because it comes from me, not because I need other peoples' approval." Another could be, "My accomplishments or failures do not determine who I am. My character and the way I treat others determines who I am."

If you are struggling with feelings of guilt or shame, remember that "habitual lying is an addiction, not a moral issue". By adopting this mindset, you will avoid getting too down on yourself.

You aren't a bad person for having a detrimental behavioral flaw, and it's very important to realize that there were many factors outside of your control that caused you to pick up the behavioral habit in the first place.

Thinking Carefully Before Speaking

Thinking carefully before speaking is a very simple, yet effective, technique. Make sure that when someone asks you a question and you are inclined to answer, take a pause and think about the answer you are about to give.

If you are not willing to answer it with a truthful statement, then make sure you are at least aware of the false statement you are going to give.

Be sure to consciously make the choice of what is true and what is false, as well as why, or why not, you decided to tell the truth in that situation. You may feel self-conscious for taking your time in conversations at first, but remember that you are doing this for the long haul.

Practice consciously thinking about what you are going to say before you open your mouth to speak. Consistently remind yourself throughout the day to "breath deeply and think before you speak". By affirming this to yourself, you'll be much less likely to impulsively lie when someone asks you a question.

A further tip that can assist in this new practice, is to imagine your lungs are lowering into your pelvis with your deep breaths. By incorporating this deep form of breathing into your daily life, you'll notice that panic and nervousness will tend to dissipate, allowing you to communicate without as much fear.

While practicing this behavior daily will help you to maintain a more relaxed and less fearful state, remember to also do this when in conversation with others or when just hanging out in a group setting.

If you are the one speaking, practice talking slower and with more pauses in your speech - especially when you are recalling stories or talking about topics that you aren't the most comfortable talking about. This will allow you to be more conscious of your behavior and you'll be surprised at how effective it is.

While you practice changing the way you breath, think, and speak in conversation, you can also work on the way you listen. When the people around you are speaking on a subject that you have little to no knowledge about, recognize it and consciously listen to them speak.

Slowly work to eliminate speaking when you are ignorant on a subject. Depending on the way you've been communicating in the past, this can dramatically lower the lies you create and the chance of you making up a story.

On a similar note, practice admitting ignorance when someone questions you about a topic that you're not knowledgeable about. By combining these two tips, you'll jump into less conversations with a false story and you'll make up less lies when someone is questioning you directly.

Journaling

You should record all of the lies, as well as the "hard truths", that you tell throughout the day. Consciously explore the circumstances surrounding those behaviors, including your emotional state, the setting, time of day, etc. By doing this consistently, you'll start to recognize the patterns and triggers for your behavior.

You may realize that you tend to be dishonest when you are stressed or around a certain family member. From there, you can start to work on why you may have become that way and how to go about preventing/improving those situations in the future.

While journaling, you should also identify which aspects of your life you want to be more honest about, in order. Start by delving into which aspects of your life you are most and least confident about, as well as the aspects of your life that you are most and least honest about. Try to get as specific as possible.

Remember that journaling can be done in many different ways and you can do as much or as little as you want - but there are some important principles that can guide you in this process. View every lie and truth as being important. Do not let "small lies" pass.

Keep a high personal standard of eventually, one day, being truthful in all aspects of your life. View letting small lies pass as an avalanche that will compound over time, if you don't nip it in the bud.

Your Ideal Life

This may sound counter-intuitive, but a tip that might help you out is to work on creating a life that your current self wants to lie about. When you communicate with others, what are the things that you want to tell them about yourself?

Try to identify which areas of your life that you feel like you're "slacking" in. Ideally, what kind of person would you like to be? What are the traits that you respect in others?

Define these things as well as you can, and then come up with a short-term and long-term game plan to help you slowly become that person. If you do not have the traits that you desire yet, then you now have an idea regarding the aspects of your life that you need to work on.

Also, keep in mind that you have to keep your expectations realistic. If you think that you need more time to work on a skill or a trait, then do not be too hard on yourself. Trim down your larger, more difficult goals to more actionable ones so you can observe yourself making progress.

By becoming the person who possesses the traits that you value in others, you'll slowly start to see your self-esteem grow and you'll inevitably start to become a person that you feel PROUD of being.

Know Who to Trust

One very important aspect of an effective treatment program is being honest with your therapist, family, and friends. Even if you cannot tell them everything, at least be truthful about your answers. If you feel more comfortable telling them a lie, instead tell them that you aren't comfortable talking about it at the moment.

While you may be aware that you have difficulty telling the truth to people around you because you have fears that they may not be able to accept who you really are or the things you can really do, remember that what they think about your life does not really matter.

You will not be able to have control of everyone's perception of the truth, but it is not a burden that you should carry. You only need to be concerned about what you truly think of yourself.

At the same time, keep in mind that while you may have doubts about what people may think about you once you start telling the truth, those who are there to support you during your journey to recovery more likely trust your ability to succeed in changing the habits in your life.

Also, remember that when these people trust you, they are also more likely to know that you have been lying to them all along. However, that did not stop them from building their trust on your commitment to change. Work on that trust and think that it should motivate you – maybe you just need to reciprocate that trust for you to change your life.

This will go a long way in building up the honesty in your mind, and it will help those around you to understand that you are working on yourself and not just blowing them off with another lie.

It's None of Their Business - Or Is It?

Everyone has their own right to privacy and in some cases you might think that your problem with lying is your business alone. However, pathological lying can have an impact on every relationship that a person is involved in. Anyone who has to put up with the negative consequences of your behavior deserves to know the truth.

That also means that you are not alone in your journey to recovery – you are doing it together with the people whom you have lied to in the past, as well as those who remain on your side.

They Cannot Cope With The Truth

Pathological liars may keep their behavior from their loved ones simply because they think that those people will not be able to cope with the truth. In reality, it will be much more frustrating for them to deal with your behavior if they are aware of your pathological tendencies and you continue to lie to them.

Telling people the truth will not only help you break your addiction to lying, but also allow others to heal from the damage that lies bring. Once you are able to tell the truth to others, you cannot expect them to immediately be able to deal with the situation.

However, you can trust that eventually, people will be able to forgive you for lying and cope with any loss that they may have incurred because of your previous inability to tell the truth. By not delaying the truth from people, they can plan their lives better and allow them to live without high expectations from you. This prevents both parties from exerting too much pressure on each other.

Criticism from Loved Ones

There is no doubt that some of the people whom you choose to tell the truth to will become upset. You might also hear some comments that aren't intended to be criticism, but you could perceive them as such. It is important to know the difference between the two.

At this point, you have to be objective on what people say about you once you start telling the truth. You have to understand that they don't mean to pressure you, but they have been accustomed to a particular set of beliefs that they may be willing to change in time.

Soon enough, they will be able to give out well-informed opinions about the things that you can truly do. After all, the people who surround you now are those who want the best for you, despite the things that you may have said or done before.

Try to realize that people who truly care about your well-being will want what is best for you. It might take some adjustments, but they can also be a great source of encouragement in overcoming your pathological lying issues.

Chapter 7:

Road to Recovery

Even people who have learned to overcome their negative behaviors may develop feelings of guilt after realizing the damage they have caused to the people around them.

This can place a heavy burden on a person's shoulders and that person will never fully recover from the effects of pathological lying if they do not learn to forgive themselves. Let's explore some important concepts for recovery!

Be Accountable For Your Actions

Accountability is one thing that most people expect from a person who does not tell the truth. Once you recognize that lying may cause hurt to others or to yourself, you need to keep in mind that you have full control over your choices.

This means that when you choose to tell a lie, you have to be prepared for the consequences of your actions.

Practice Apologizing

Whenever you catch yourself telling a lie, quickly correct your statement even if it means changing your story. This will help you become more apologetic and truthful. Do not worry about what people think about you – your friends and loved ones will be able to understand you better if you tell them that your story is not as marvelous as you think it should be. They will be better aware of your situation and accept you for who you are.

Also, remember that you have no way of truly predicting what is going on in another person's mind. While it is likely that some people will voice out frustration or look surprised once you start telling the truth, you need to keep in mind that these are normal reactions.

It is also quite likely that people will just brush off any blunder that you have made, or just laugh it off. You will also start feeling better when you find out that nothing terrible will happen when you tell the truth.

Learn to Forgive Yourself

Forgiving one's self is one of the essential, yet most difficult, parts of recovery for some people. When you begin to trust the truth that you can be who you really are and that there is no real pressure for you to become a person that people may wish you'd be, you will be able to realize that accepting that you are capable of making mistakes will allow you to improve yourself. There are times when you may feel that you are not in control, but that happens to everyone.

If you feel that things should have happened differently and you could have acted different in a situation, let it go. Do not worry about things that you cannot change. You have your life ahead of you and once you are motivated to become the better version of yourself, you will realize that the opinion of other people does not matter.

What you need to work on is your opinion of YOURSELF. Give yourself the chance to heal and work at your own pace. If you think that people will be not so kind to you once you start becoming true to yourself, then exert that kindness to yourself instead.

Many of the factors involved in you becoming a compulsive liar were not in your control. You must remember that you are trying your best now and that is all that matters today, tomorrow, and for the rest of your life.

Meditation and Reflection

Meditation can be an extremely helpful tool for the personal healing process, as well as for increasing self-awareness. You might not be able to change the past, but you can certainly do something about the future. There are many forms of meditation, but all of them involve not restricting your feelings.

Through meditation, you will be able to live more in the moment, without the minor anxieties that can arise in modern life, along with learning how to channel your energy and focus.

Set aside at least ten minutes each day to meditate. Begin by taking deep breaths and allow any feelings of guilt or frustration to come into your mind. Your goal will be to realize that guilt is only a feeling that comes along with pathological lying and that it does not dictate who you are as a person. Notice the feelings that arise, but don't get attached to them so far as to let them define your character.

Mantra

Historically, mantras were used by religious people, and some chant them on a regular basis. You can also develop your own mantra and then practice saying it every day. An example would be something like: "I am already free of pathological lying" or "I forgive myself".

This may feel awkward at first, but this can change your thought patterns over time because you begin to see yourself as a different person.

You can think of mantras as a form of mind setting – by speaking your desires aloud, as if you have already achieved them, your subconscious will enable your body to act them out. This will help you prevent any automatic thoughts and utterances that may lead you to lie to others.

Apart from reciting mantras during the beginning of the day, you can recite them whenever you have the urge to lie or you catch yourself in the middle of one. This will make it easier for you to apologize and correct a statement, or stick to the true version of a story.

Atonement

The guilt that a pathological liar feels is his/her own way of atoning for their lies. Instead of feeling miserable, channel that energy and do therapeutic work, such as volunteering for charities.

Do Things That Inspire You

Make a list of things that make you happy. Do one thing that makes you happy as a reward for not lying, whether it is meditating, going for a run, or reading a book. Doing pleasurable things that do not involve lying will create positive reinforcement for you.

It may also be a great idea for you to start doing things that you originally liked. If you liked riding bicycles in the past and you are pretending to prefer cars now, this is your chance to go back to your old hobby. By acknowledging that you can like things without the approval of other people, you can discover things that you truly enjoy about yourself.

At the same time, you can start telling true accomplishments and information in the fields that you really are adept in. When you do that, you gain the awareness that you can feel happy when you tell true achievements, instead of the ones that you just make up as you go in the momentum of a conversation.

If You Are Being Lied To.... (And Want to Help)

If you are a person that is being compulsively lied to by someone that you care about, you must first realize that the lying behavior is not necessarily to be taken personal.

If someone compulsively lies to you, their personal values and behaviors are not in alignment with someone who holds honesty in high regards. By looking at it this way, you will be more understanding of their struggles.

We must first understand that the term "lying" should not automatically be associated with the word "bad", especially in this context of habitual, repetitive behavior. Though it may be hard to believe for those who are being lied to, lying is not always a conscious process, especially for those who picked up the habit in early childhood.

Keep in mind that people lie to get something that they want and avoid things that may hurt them. If you are aware that a person is lying to you, it would be wise to talk to him/her in private and tell them that you are aware that he/she is not telling the truth.

While the other person may deny it initially, telling him/her about your awareness will give them an idea that he/she will not be able to keep lying to others all the time. This will give them the idea that he/she is bound to get caught, and it would be better for them to correct the act before it is too late.

People who have limited experience around compulsive liars may also find it hard to believe that the liar is not consciously selective in who he/she lies to, or malicious in his/her intent. Rather, they usually lie when talking about topics that they feel inadequate about. In other words, whether it be a stranger or their own mother, a compulsive liar (and/or person with low self-esteem) will probably feel self-conscious about that specific area of their life.

Instead of dealing with the truth of where they are at, the person will try to fabricate an "alternate truth" to protect themselves from (perceived) potential pain or awkwardness.

While dealing with compulsive liars is definitely a task that requires patience, sympathy, and understanding, you should also not allow yourself to be used as a doormat. Give yourself space and be stern in what you will and won't accept as a behavior in your inter-personal relationship. This will help you and the compulsive liar in the long run.

Conclusion

I worked hard on creating the best guide for "compulsive/pathological liars" that I could. These are all the strategies and information that has worked for me, as well as others that I have talked to and researched. I guarantee that if you stay consistent, these strategies will work for you as well. Be optimistic about your current situation and make small progress each day!

Remember that every person struggles with their own issues. Some people have gambling addictions, some have trouble eating a healthy diet, and others have physical disabilities. The important thing to note is that nobody is inherently better than anyone else, and we can all learn to live with the hand we were dealt.

Do not feel inferior if you suffer from compulsive lying or low self-esteem. You have an uphill battle ahead of you in order to overcome your issues, but as long as you keep a long-term perspective and focus on the person you CAN become, then things will work out for you.

Good luck in your own journey!

Made in the USA
Las Vegas, NV
19 October 2023

79306290R00075